SHIRLEY WILLIS was born in Glasgow, Scotland. She has worked as an illustrator, designer and editor, mainly on books for children.

BETTY ROOT was the Director of the Reading and Language Information Centre at the University of Reading, England, for over twenty years. She has worked on numerous children's books, both fiction and non-fiction.

PETER LAFFERTY is a former secondary school science teacher. Since 1985 he has been a full-time author of science and technology books for children and family audiences. He has edited and contributed to many scientific encyclopedias and dictionaries.

BOOK EDITOR: KAREN BARKER SMITH
TECHNICAL CONSULTANT: PETER LAFFERTY
LANGUAGE CONSULTANT: BETTY ROOT

AN SBC BOOK, CONCEIVED, EDITED AND DESIGNED BY
THE SALARIYA BOOK COMPANY, 25, MARLBOROUGH PLACE,
BRIGHTON, EAST SUSSEX BN1 1UB, UNITED KINGDOM.
© THE SALARIYA BOOK COMPANY LTD MCMXCIX

ISBN 978 0 531 11827 6 (LIB. BDG.)
ISBN 978 0 531 15977 4 (PBK.)

VISIT FRANKLIN WATTS ON THE INTERNET AT:
HTTP://PUBLISHING.GROLIER.COM

GROLIER
PUBLISHING

A catalog record for this title is available from the Library of Congress.

ALL RIGHTS RESERVED.
PRINTED IN SHANGHAI, CHINA.
REPRINTED IN 2012.
18 19 20 R 15 14 13 12

WHIZ KIDS

CONTENTS

Wherever you see this sign, ask an adult to help you.

WHIZ KIDS
TELL ME HOW MUCH IT WEIGHS

Written and
illustrated by
SHIRLEY WILLIS

W
FRANKLIN WATTS
A Division of Grolier Publishing

NEW YORK • LONDON • HONG KONG • SYDNEY
DANBURY, CONNECTICUT

IS IT HEAVY... OR LIGHT?

An elephant is heavy, but a feather is light. They each weigh a different amount. Everything can be weighed — even air.

A feather is so light, it seems weightless. Try holding a feather in one hand and a cushion stuffed with feathers in the other. If there are lots of feathers, you can feel how much they weigh.

THE WEIGHT OF SOMETHING IS — HOW HEAVY IT IS!

7

IS IT HARD TO LIFT?

Weight makes an object
easy or hard to lift.
A light object is easy to lift
— it does not weigh
very much.
A heavy object is hard to lift
— it weighs a lot.

This bone is light.
It's easy to lift.

8

This bag is heavy.
It's hard to lift.

This box is too heavy
to lift.

GRUNT!

DOES IT LOOK HEAVY?

A big object can look heavy,
but is it?
It can be light.

Size and weight are
different measurements.
Size only shows
how big an object is,
not how much it weighs.

THIS BOX IS HEAVIER
THAN IT LOOKS!

THIS BOX IS EMPTY — IT'S LIGHTER THAN IT LOOKS

DOES BIG EQUAL HEAVY?

You will need: Three different-sized boxes (one small, one medium, and one large)
Some marbles
Adhesive tape

1. Count how many marbles it takes to fill the smallest box. Tape it shut.
2. Put half as many marbles into the medium-sized box. Tape it shut.
3. Put one marble into the biggest box. Tape it shut.

Now test your friends. Ask them to guess which box is heaviest.

WHICH IS HEAVIER?

Before weighing machines were invented, people had to guess if an object was heavy or light.

WHICH IS HEAVIER —
A TON OF FEATHERS
OR A TON OF BRICKS?

A ton is a set measure of weight — it never changes. So, a ton of feathers weighs exactly the same as a ton of bricks.

CAN YOU GUESS?

You will need: Objects of
different sizes
and weights
Two shopping bags

Put one object in each bag.
Now ask a friend to lift up
both bags to guess
which is heavier.

When two weights
are almost the same,
it is much harder
to tell which
is heavier.

1. Start with a heavy object in one
   bag and a light one in the other.
2. Next, choose two objects that are
   closer in weight than before.
3. Finally, choose two objects that
   weigh almost the same.

?

IS IT LIGHTER?

IS IT HEAVIER?

— IT'S HARD
TO TELL!

13

DOES IT WEIGH THE SAME?

Balance is a simple way
to see if two objects
weigh the same or not.

This end of the
see-saw drops
because I am heavier.

THUD!

This end of the see-saw has gone up because I am lighter.

If the girl and the dog each weighed the same, the see-saw would balance. Each end would be the same distance off the ground.

MAKE A BALANCE SCALE

You will need: 1 wire coat hanger
2 paper plates
Adhesive tape
4 pieces of wool
(equal lengths)

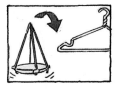

1. Turn both plates upside down.
2. Tape the ends of two pieces of wool to the bottom of each plate (as shown).
3. Loop the wool over the coat hanger (as shown).

15

HOW DO YOU WEIGH IT?

16

YOU CAN HAVE 5 MARBLES WORTH OF BISCUITS EVERY DAY!

You can measure out exact amounts by using a set of weights.

WOOF!

You can use any objects as weights as long as they are all the same. Marbles, building blocks, or pebbles will do.

HOW MUCH DOES IT WEIGH?

You will need: Some marbles
Sand
Paper clips
Small pieces of paper

1. Choose the number of marbles to use.
2. Measure out enough sand to balance the marbles. Now do the same with the paper clips and the paper. Is each pile the same size?

Each pile weighs the same but is a different size. The lightest material makes the biggest pile because it takes more to balance the marbles.

You can balance the marbles with anything. The lighter an object is, the more you need to balance the marbles. The heavier it is, the less you need. (It takes a lot of feathers to balance two marbles but not many paper clips.)

THERE MUST BE AN AWFUL LOT OF FEATHERS IN A TON!

17

HOW MUCH DOES IT WEIGH?

When everyone used different weights to measure, no one agreed about the weight of anything.

The United States uses a system of measurement based on ounces and pounds.

How heavy is this book you are reading?
Would it be weighed in ounces, pounds, or tons?

(In ounces.)

Hard candies are light. They are weighed in ounces (oz).

I am heavier. I am weighed in pounds (lbs).

I am really heavy. I am weighed in tons.

19

How Heavy Are You?

We weigh ourselves
on a bathroom scale.

If you don't eat properly,
you can weigh too much
or too little.
It is best
not to be
too fat or
too thin.

MAKE A WEIGHT CHART

You will need: Bathroom scale
                 Thumbtacks
                 Scissors
                 Ruler
                 Two sheets of paper

1. Pin one sheet of paper to the wall.
2. Divide the other sheet into equal strips using the ruler. Then cut them up.
3. Weigh yourself.
4. Place your strip of paper beside the measuring scale shown on this page (right).
   Mark your weight on the strip with a dotted line.
5. Cut along the dotted line.
6. Write your name and weight on the strip and pin it to the wall chart.
   Ask your classmates to do the same.

Who is heaviest? Who is lightest?
Find out how much your class weighs by adding everyone's weight together.

MEASURING SCALE IN POUNDS

84
70
56
42
28
14
0

WHY DO WE WEIGH THINGS?

There are many reasons to find out how much something weighs.

WE WEIGH OURSELVES

We weigh babies and children to see if they are growing well. Adults must weigh themselves to check that they are a healthy weight too.

22

WE WEIGH FOOD

Most of the food we buy is weighed so we can choose how much we need. Sometimes food is weighed in handy amounts before we buy it.

THIS PACKAGE IS BIG, BUT I'M GLAD IT DOESN'T WEIGH MUCH!

WE WEIGH PACKAGES

We weigh packages and letters at the post office. A heavy package costs more to mail than a light one.

23

IS WEIGHT IMPORTANT?

Weight is important for safety.

A plane can be too heavy to fly.

A bridge can break if there is too much weight on it.

IS IT SAFE?

You will need: Two drinking straws
Two building blocks

1. Make a simple bridge with straws and building blocks as shown.
2. Place a coin in the middle of the bridge. Add as many coins as you can and watch what happens.

When the coins become too heavy for the bridge, it will collapse.

A boat can sink if its load is too heavy.

TOO MANY CHILDREN WILL SINK THE BOAT!

IS IT SAFE?

The boat gets heavier as each child climbs aboard. As it gets heavier, the boat sinks deeper into the water. This boat is not safe because it is overloaded — it might sink.

25

HOW HEAVY IS AN ELEPHANT?

WHOOSH!

We weigh ourselves on bathroom scales. An elephant is too heavy for these scales, and a feather is too light.

YOU MUST BE TOO LIGHT FOR BATHROOM SCALES, TOO!

Very heavy and very light weights are measured on different types of scales.

AN ELEPHANT CAN WEIGH 6 TONS!

An adult male African elephant is the heaviest animal on land.

27

HOW HEAVY IS THE EARTH?

The earth weighs a huge amount —
many millions of tons.
It's hard to imagine so much weight.

AN ELEPHANT IS HEAVY — IT WEIGHS AS MUCH AS
90 ADULT HUMANS, BUT...

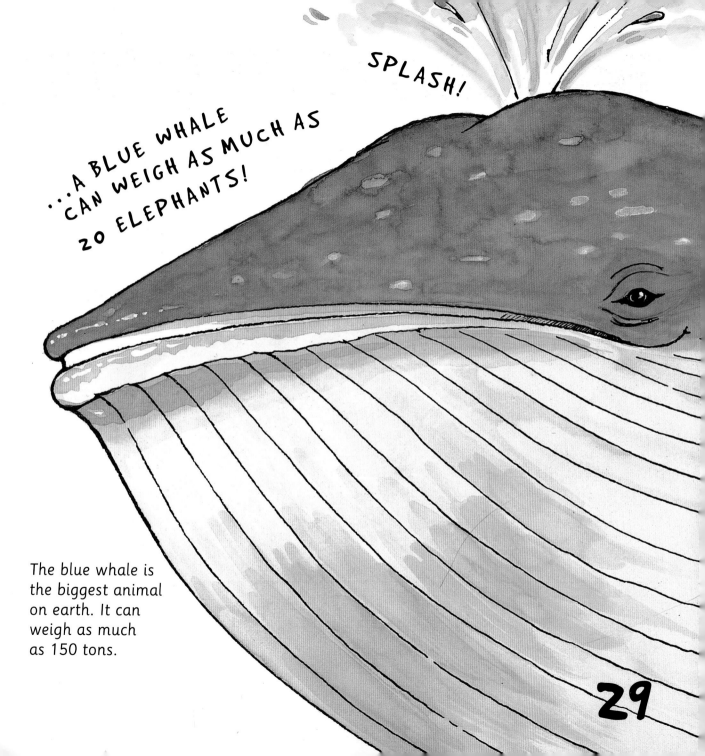

SPLASH!

...A BLUE WHALE CAN WEIGH AS MUCH AS 20 ELEPHANTS!

The blue whale is the biggest animal on earth. It can weigh as much as 150 tons.

29

GLOSSARY

balance — When one weight is equal to another.

balance scale — A simple weighing machine that balances one weight against another.

heavy — When an object weighs a lot.

light — When an object doesn't weigh very much.

load — The amount of weight to be carried.

ounce — A unit of weight that is used to measure small amounts.

pound — A unit of weight equal to 16 ounces.

size — How big or how small an object is.

ton — A unit of weight equal to 2,000 pounds.

weight — How heavy an object is.

INDEX

U.S. $5.95
CAN. $8.50

WHIZ KIDS

TELL ME HOW MUCH IT WEIGHS

INTRODUCING THE **WHIZ KIDS.**
JOIN THIS GROUP OF FRIENDS AT THE BEGINNING
OF AN ADVENTURE – DISCOVERING WHAT
AN EXCITING WORLD WE LIVE IN.

THIS BOOK ANSWERS THE WHIZ KIDS' QUESTIONS ABOUT
WEIGHT, HOW AND WHY THINGS ARE WEIGHED
AND THE UNITS OF MEASUREMENT USED.

INCLUDES **FUN EXPERIMENTS** AND
THINGS TO **MAKE** AND **DO.**

WHIZ KIDS TITLES:

ISBN 0-531-15977-9

9 780531 159774

A FRANKLIN WATTS BOOK